T0085548

PUBLISHED BY
Wise Publications

EXCLUSIVE DISTRIBUTORS
Music Sales Corporation
257 Park Avenue South, New York, NY 10010, USA.
Music Sales Limited
8/9 Frith Street, London W1D 3JB, England.
Music Sales Pty Limited
120 Rothschild Avenue, Rosebery,
NSW 2018, Australia.

Order No. MFA10012
ISBN 0-8256-7551-0
This book © Copyright 2006 Wise Publications,
a division of Music Sales Corporation.

DESIGNED AND PACKAGED BY
Balley Design Associates
CREATIVE DIRECTOR **Simon Balley**
DESIGNER **Karen Hood**
PROJECT EDITOR **Hilary Mandleberg**

All animal images copyright
Digital Vision and Getty Images

Manufactured in Peru.

CD CREDITS
Executive producer: Akira Komatsu
Composition: Hiroki Sakaguchi
Performance: Hiroki Sakaguchi (Keyboard), Chikara Suda
(Cello & Gutstring), Shigeru Oikawa (Recorder/Traverso),
Tohru Sakurada (Lute), Hiroshi Fukuzawa (viola da gamba),
Takeshi Ishikawa (percussion)
Engineer: Teruaki Igarashi (bazooka Studio & Paradise
Studio 2003 Spring)
Co-operation: Azabu Veterinary University Man & Animal
Relationship Research Team (+ Sakura, Layna and Kuro)
Total planning: Satoshi Yoshida (Shinko Music)
Notes: Some of the tracks in this CD contain sounds that are
only audible to animals

dog daze...

Wise Publications
part of The Music Sales Group
London / New York / Paris / Sydney / Copenhagen / Berlin / Madrid / Tokyo

How beautiful it is
to do nothing,
and then rest
afterwards.

I shall never forget that the probability of a **miracle**,

though infinitesimally small...

6

...is not exactly zero.

Beware of silent dogs
and still waters.

I've **tried** relaxing, but...

... I don't know...

I feel **more** comfortable

tense.

A well-spent day
brings happy sleep.

I love deadlines.

I like the **whooshing** sound they make as they fly by.

I shall always decide not to decide, unless of course I decide to change my mind.

Sleep is a symptom of

caffeine deprivation.

Facts quite often …

put me to sleep at noon.

To accomplish great things,
we must **dream** as well as act.

I firmly believe that tomorrow holds the possibility

for new technologies, astounding discoveries,

and a reprieve from my obligations.

People who say they sleep like a baby...... usually don't have one.

What's the use of worrying?
It never **was** worthwhile.

Laziness is nothing **more** than the
habit of resting before you get tired.

29

No matter **how** much pressure
you feel at work,
if you could find ways to relax
for at least five minutes
every hour,
you'd be more productive.

I believe that if anything is worth doing,

it would have been
done already.

If at first I don't succeed,

there is always next year.

Nothing can bring you

peace

but yourself.

If you're going to do something tonight that you'll be sorry for tomorrow morning, sleep late.

I have never taken
any exercise except
sleeping and resting.

Idleness is only a coarse name for my infinite capacity for living in the present.

If a man insisted always on being serious, and never allowed himself a bit of fun and relaxation, he would go mad or become unstable

without knowing it.

It is **better** to have loafed
and lost
than never to have loafed
at all.

Learning to ignore things is one of the great paths to inner peace.

Sleep is when all the unsorted **stuff** comes flying out as from a dustbin upset in a **high** wind.

Seek home for rest,
For home is best.

Stress is an ignorant state.

It believes that everything is an emergency.

Nothing is that important.

Idleness is
an appendix to
nobility.

I don't know why it is we are in such a hurry to get up when we fall down.

You might think we would lie there and rest for a while.

The **time** to relax is when you don't have time for it.

I will **become** a member
of the ancient Order of
Two-Headed Turtles (the
Procrastinator's Society)

if they ever get it
organized.

There is **nothing** like dreams to create the future.

The main thing to do is
relax
and let your talent
do the work.

Laugh and the world laughs with you;
snore and you sleep alone.

I will never rush into a job
without a lifetime
of consideration.

To his dog, every man is Napoleon; hence the constant popularity of dogs.

No **rest** is worth anything
except the rest
that is **earned**.

He felt that his whole life was
some kind of dream and he
sometimes wondered whose it was...

...and whether they were
enjoying it.

Remain calm, serene,

always in command of yourself.

You will then find out

how easy it is to get along.

Life
is a
Dream.

A life of peace,
purity, and
refinement
leads to a calm
and untroubled
old age.

It is not good
a sleeping hound
to wake.

I obey the law of **inverse** excuses which demands that the **greater** the task to be done, the more **insignificant** the work that must be done prior to **beginning** the greater task.

Nature does not hurry,
yet everything is accomplished.

Ambition is a poor excuse for not having sense enough to be lazy.

Good friends ...
and a **sleepy conscience;**

this is the **ideal** life.

I will never put off until tomorrow,

what I can forget about

forever.

who said what?

p.4 Spanish proverb; p.6 Anonymous; p.8 Portuguese proverb; p.10 Anonymous; p.13 Leonardo da Vinci; p.14 Douglas Adams; p.16 Anonymous; p.18 Anonymous; p.21 Ray Bradbury; p.22 Anatole France; p.25 Anonymous; p.27 Leo J. Burke; p.29 George Asaf (above); Mortimer Caplan (below); p.31 Dr. Joyce Brothers; p.32 Anonymous; p.35 Anonymous; p.36 Ralph Waldo Emerson; p.39 Henny Youngman; p.40 Mark Twain; p.43 Cyril Connolly; p.45 Herodotus; p.47 James Thurber; p.49 Robert J. Sawyer; p.51 William Golding; p.53 Thomas Tusser; p.55 Natalie Goldberg; p.56 Robert Burton; p.58 Max Eastman ; p.61 Sydney J. Harris; p.63 Anonymous; p.64 Victor Hugo; p.67 Charles Barkley; p.68 Anthony Burgess; p.70 Anonymous; p.72 Aldous Huxley; p.75 Jean Paul; p.77 Douglas Adams; p.79 Paramahansa Yogananda; p.81 Pedro Calderón de la Barca; p.82 Cicero; p.84 Geoffrey Chaucer; p.86 Anonymous; p.89 Lao-tzu; p.91 Milan Kundera; p.93 Mark Twain; p.94 Anonymous

Every effort has been made to contact or trace all copyright holders. In future editions the publishers will be glad to make good any errors or omissions that are brought to their attention.

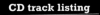

CD track listing

1 / Morning Nap Time **2 /** Touch Me Softly
3 / Rainy Day Dream **4 /** With My Master

All tracks: (Hiroki Sakaguchi) Shinko Music Publishing Co., Ltd.

Also available: cat naps... MFA10011 ISBN 0-8256-7550-2